My Listen and Learn Bible

Is Presented To

_____

On

_____

By

_____

My Listen
And Learn
BIBLE

Illustrated by David Barnett

Chariot Books
A Divsion of Cook Communications

Chariot Books™
is an imprint of David C. Cook Publishing Co.
David C. Cook Publishing Co., Elgin, Illinois 60120
David C. Cook Publishing Co., Weston, Ontario
Kingsway Communications, Eastbourne, England

MY LISTEN AND LEARN BIBLE

© 1994 David C. Cook Publishing Co. for text and illustrations.

Cover designed by Larry Taylor
Edited by Lori Davis
First Printing, 1994
Printed in the United States of America
98 97 96 95 94 5 4 3 2 1

A Note to Grown-ups:

Reading the Bible can be one of the best experiences in a young child's life.

The Bible teaches children important truths that they will carry with them for a lifetime. The Bible introduces children to the God who loves them so much.

My Listen and Learn Bible retells some of the world's most beloved stories—from the story of Creation to Paul's missionary travels.

Children will love looking at the beautiful illustrations and will ask you to read these time-tested favorites again and again.

Table of Contents
Old Testament

New Testament

God Made Everything

Once there was nothing. God made the heavens and the earth. He made the sun and moon and stars. He gathered the waters together and separated them from the dry land. Then God made every kind of plant, and creatures that walk and swim and fly.

But God was not finished. He needed someone to care for His beautiful world. So God made a man and named him Adam. Then God made a woman to be Adam's friend and helper. Adam named her Eve.

God gave Adam and Eve their own special garden, called Eden. God told them to take care of the beautiful world He made. Everything God made was very good!

Based on Genesis 1:1-31; 2:8-23; 3:20
Value: Praise

Adam and Eve Sin

Adam and Eve lived in the beautiful garden God made. One day God said, "The fruit in the garden is for you to eat. But one tree is special. Do not eat from it. If you do, I will punish you."

A snake was also in the garden. Satan talked through the snake to Eve. Satan said, "Did God tell you not to eat the fruit from the special tree? You won't be punished," said Satan. "You will know what God knows."

Eve looked at the tree. The fruit looked so good! She wanted to know everything God knows. So Eve ate the fruit. She gave some to Adam. He ate the fruit too.

God came to talk to them, but they hid. They were afraid because they hadn't obeyed God. He said, "Because you didn't obey Me, I must punish you." God sent Adam and Eve out of the garden. God said, "You must work hard now. You will not always be happy."

Based on Genesis 3
Value: Conviction

Noah Obeys God

One day God looked at the world He made. He saw people everywhere doing bad things. God said, "I am going to start the world over again. I will send rain to cover the earth."

God told Noah to build a big boat. He worked hard for many days, and at last it was ready. Then God said, "Take two of every animal into the boat. Take your family. Take enough food for everyone." When everything was ready, Noah and his family went inside and God shut the door.

God sent rain for forty days and nights. Noah and his family and all the animals were safe because Noah did what God told him to do.

Based on Genesis 6:14-22; 7:11-24
Value: Obedience

Abraham Gets a Promise from God

Abraham and Sarah loved each other. But something was missing in their lives. They had no children, and they were very sad.

So God promised them a son the next year. When Abraham heard this, he worshiped God. But inside he was laughing. "Me—a father?" he said to himself. "I'll be a hundred years old, and Sarah will be ninety!"

God knew that Abraham laughed, so He told Abraham to name the baby *Isaac*, which means laughter.

Abraham and Sarah waited and waited and a year later baby Isaac was born, just as God had promised. Now they were happy. God had given them a son.

Based on Genesis 17:15-19; 21:1-5
Value: Patience

Jacob Tricks His Father

Isaac was growing old, so he said, "I will bless you, Esau, before I die. But first bring me some deer meat." So Esau went hunting for a deer.

While he was gone, his brother Jacob got some goat meat and had it cooked for Isaac. His mother put goatskins on Jacob's arms so that he felt hairy like Esau. Then he went to his father and said, "I am Esau. I have some meat for you. I want you to bless me now."

Isaac felt Jacob's arms. He thought it was Esau. So Isaac blessed Jacob. Then Esau came home with deer meat. He asked his father to bless him.

"Who are you?" asked Isaac.

"I am your son, Esau."

Isaac said, "Your brother has tricked me and taken your blessing. I have no blessing left for you." Esau was very angry. Jacob ran far away from his family. He knew he couldn't come back for a long time.

Based on Genesis 27:1-45
Value: Honesty

Joseph Forgives His Brothers

Joseph was Jacob's favorite son. Jacob's other sons were jealous. They sold Joseph to traders going to Egypt.

But God was with Joseph. God warned Joseph that in seven years no crops would grow anywhere. Joseph became the king's most trusted helper. Joseph helped the people of Egypt save up plenty of food for the bad times ahead.

The rest of the world was hungry—including Joseph's own family. When they came to Egypt for food, Joseph had a choice to make. Would he forgive them or let them go hungry?

Joseph hugged them all. "God turned into good what you meant for bad. This way, I have helped many people. Don't be afraid. Come live with me in Egypt where you will have plenty of food."

Joseph made a hard choice—but the right choice!

Based on Genesis 37:3-28; 41:1—42:6; 45:1-11
Value: Forgiveness

Miriam Saves Baby Moses

Miriam had an important job. She watched her baby brother, Moses, floating on the river in a basket. Their family had hidden him there so the mean king of Egypt wouldn't find him.

Miriam saw the king's daughter come down to the river to take a bath. The princess found Moses crying. She felt sorry for him and picked him up. Miriam ran to the princess and asked, "Shall I find someone to take care of the baby for you?"

The princess said yes. She needed someone to help. So Miriam brought her mother to care for the baby. Moses would be safe, thanks to his big sister, Miriam!

Based on Exodus 2:1-10
Value: Courage

Moses Crosses the Red Sea

Moses loved God. God chose Moses to lead His people into a new country. God had a new home for them.

Before long, Moses stopped by a big sea. The people cried, "How can we cross the sea? Now we will never get to our new home."

God told Moses, "Hold your arms over the sea. I will make the water move apart." All night God split the water with a strong wind. Then Moses and the people and all their animals walked across on dry ground.

The people shouted, "Hurray! God has helped us. Now we can go to our new home."

Based on Exodus 14:15, 16, 21, 22, 31
Value: Trust

God Gives Food

Moses was leading God's people to a new land. To get there, they had to walk across a hot desert. They would travel for many years.

The journey seemed long. No food grew in the desert sand, and the people had eaten everything they had brought along. The people started to doubt God and complain. "Did God lead us here just so we could die of hunger? Where will we get food?"

God told Moses, "In the evening I will send meat. In the morning I will send bread."

Every evening God sent big birds called quail. There was meat for everyone.

Every morning God sent bread called manna. The people gathered it off the ground. Everyone had just enough to eat. They did not need to doubt God's care for them.

Based on Exodus 16:3-18
Value: Trust

The Ten Commandments

Moses called to the people, "Come here! Come here! God has special rules for us. He gave us these rules because He knows that obeying Him is the way to be happy."

The most important rule came first: Love God more than anything else. Then God said there would be one day each week to worship Him. Another of God's special rules was just for children. This rule told children to love and obey their parents. God also said that people must not steal or lie or hurt others.

God wrote His rules on tablets made of stone. They were not just for those who followed Moses. God made them to help everyone know how to obey Him and be happy.

Based on Exodus 20:1-17
Value: Obedience

Ruth Helps Naomi

Ruth loved her mother-in-law, Naomi. She promised to follow Naomi anywhere. But when they moved to Naomi's hometown, they had no farm—and no food. So Ruth gathered the grain that farm workers left behind.

One day the owner of a field came to watch the workers. Boaz saw Ruth. He knew she worked hard to care for Naomi, who was too old to gather her own grain. Boaz filled Ruth's arms with extra grain.

Later Boaz said, "Ruth, will you marry me?" She said yes!

God rewarded Ruth because she cared for Naomi. Ruth had a son named Obed who later became the grandfather of David, King of Israel!

Based on Ruth 2—4
Value: Respectfulness

Samuel Listens to God

As a boy, Samuel helped Eli in the temple. Someday Samuel would be God's minister in Israel. But first he had to learn to hear God's voice.

"Samuel! Samuel!" a voice called out to him.

Samuel ran to Eli's side, but Eli said, "I didn't call you. Go back to bed."

This happened three times. At last Eli understood. "Samuel, the Lord is speaking to you. Next time say, 'Yes, Lord, I'm listening.' " So Samuel went back to bed.

The Lord called again, "Samuel! Samuel!"

This time Samuel said, "Yes, Lord, I'm listening."

As Samuel grew, the people listened when he spoke. They knew Samuel heard God's voice and obeyed Him.

Based on I Samuel 3:1-10, 19
Value: Prayerfulness

God Chooses
David to Be King

King Saul disobeyed God once too often. God said, "Saul, I will give your kingdom to someone who obeys Me."

God sent Samuel to bless the new king. Samuel thought it would be the oldest of Jesse's sons but God said no. "People look at the outside. I see inside. This isn't the man," God said.

Samuel met seven sons. To each one, God said no. Samuel asked Jesse if he had any more sons. Jesse told him that his youngest son, David, was watching the sheep. "Call him right away," Samuel said.

When David came, God told Samuel, "This is the one!" So Samuel poured special oil on David's head. David would be the next king of Israel.

Based on I Samuel 16:1-13
Value: Holiness

David and Goliath

David visited his brothers in King Saul's army. "Why are you sitting?" David asked.

"No one will fight our enemy, Goliath. He's too big and strong," they said.

"I will fight him!" David said.

King Saul thought David was too young to fight. But David was sure he could win. He picked up his sling and five smooth stones and walked toward the giant. Goliath laughed when he saw David.

David said, "I don't need a sword or spear, I have the living God to help me."

David put a stone in his sling and shot it right into Goliath's forehead. Down Goliath fell! David saved the day because he trusted in God.

Based on I Samuel 17:17-53
Value: Confidence

Jonathan Helps David

King Saul had a son named Jonathan. Jonathan and David were best friends. But the king was jealous of David and didn't want him to be a friend to his son. Saul even tried to kill David, but David ran away.

Jonathan heard what his father had done. "I need to help my friend," he thought. Jonathan said, "David, hide in a safe place. I will come tomorrow and give you a signal to let you know if it is safe to come to the palace."

Then Jonathan went to his father, but the king was very angry. "David must die!" Saul yelled.

Jonathan went to David's hiding place and shot arrows to warn him. "It isn't safe for you to come back now," Jonathan said. David and Jonathan cried and gave each other a hug. Even though David would have to leave, he and Jonathan would always be friends.

Based on I Samuel 20
Value: Loyalty

God Takes Care of Elijah

Ahab was a king who did not obey God. Ahab did not worship God. He worshiped an idol named Baal.

Elijah was a man who loved God. God made Elijah a prophet and gave him a message for King Ahab. Elijah said to the king, "You have done many wicked things. So God will not let it rain in your kingdom until I say so."

King Ahab was angry. He wanted to hurt Elijah. But God kept Elijah safe. God told Elijah to hide near a brook. Even though it did not rain, Elijah had water to drink. God sent birds with food for Elijah. Elijah followed God's way and was safe.

Based on I Kings 16:29—17:6
Value: Faith

Elijah Goes to Heaven

Elijah was God's prophet. He did what God told him to do. But Elijah was getting old. He knew he was going to be with God soon. God said, "I want Elisha to be My prophet after you come to live with me, Elijah."

Elijah found Elisha plowing in a field. He threw his coat around Elisha's shoulders. From that day, Elisha followed Elijah and learned how to be a good prophet.

One day Elijah asked Elisha, "What can I do for you?"

Elisha said, "I want God's power so I can do His work as you did."

Elijah said, "If you see me leave, you will have God's power."

Suddenly a chariot of horses appeared. They were on fire! A strong wind took Elijah to be with God. Elisha watched him go.

Elijah's coat fell to the ground. Elisha picked it up. Then he knew God's power was with him. Elisha was ready to do God's work.

Based on I Kings 19:19-21; II Kings 2:1-15
Value: Faith

A Servant Helps Naaman

A young servant girl said, "The nice lady I work for is so sad. Her husband, Naaman, has sores all over his body. I want to help them."

God gave her an idea. She told the lady about God's helper, Elisha, who could help her husband get healed. So Naaman left quickly to find Elisha.

When Naaman arrived, Elisha told him to wash seven times in the Jordan River. One. Two. Three. Four. Five. Six. Seven. When Naaman had washed seven times, his sores were gone!

"I am well!" shouted Naaman. "Thank You, God! Thank you, Elisha! And thanks to the little girl who helped me get better."

Based on II Kings 5:1-14
Value: Helpfulness

A Fiery Furnace

A long time ago, a king built an idol of shiny gold. "Everyone must bow down and worship the statue," the king said. So all the people bowed, except Shadrach, Meshach, and Abednego.

These three men said, "We will not bow down. For God has said, 'Don't bow down to any idols—worship only Me!'"

The king became so angry that he ordered the furnace be heated seven times hotter than before. He called for his soldiers to tie the three men up and throw them into a furnace immediately!

Then the king saw a strange sight. There were not three but four men walking around freely in the furnace. The fourth man was like an angel. They weren't burned—they didn't even smell like smoke!

"Praise be to the God of these brave men!" the king said. "For no god can do what their God does!"

Based on Daniel 3
Value: Faith

Daniel and the Lions

Daniel was King Darius's special helper. The other helpers were jealous, so they had the king make a law: pray only to King Darius or be eaten by lions. They knew Daniel prayed to God three times a day. Now he would be killed.

Daniel prayed anyway, and his enemies told the king. The king could not change any law once it was written. So Daniel was thrown to the lions.

At dawn, King Darius rushed to the lions' den. "Daniel, was your God able to keep you safe?"

"God sent an angel to shut the lions' mouths," Daniel said.

The king shouted, "Let everyone in my kingdom honor Daniel's God. He is the living God!"

Based on Daniel 6:1-28
Value: Courage

Jonah and the Big Fish

God wanted Jonah to tell the people of Nineveh to stop doing wrong things and ask God to forgive them. But Jonah hated the people of Nineveh. He wanted them to be punished! So Jonah got onto a boat going away from Nineveh.

A big storm came up on the sea and soon Jonah was in the water. God sent a big fish to save him. The fish opened its mouth and swallowed Jonah.

When Jonah prayed, God made the fish spit Jonah out onto dry land. Now Jonah wanted to obey God. He got on a boat going to Nineveh and told everyone to obey God. The people asked God to forgive them and God did!

Based on Jonah 1; 2:1, 10; 3
Value: Obedience

A Visit from an Angel

One day God sent an angel with a special message for Mary. "You are going to have a baby," the angel said. "God's own Son!" Mary could hardly believe that she had been chosen, but she promised to do whatever God said.

Joseph was surprised when he heard that Mary was going to have a baby. One night when Joseph was sleeping, an angel talked to him about it. "Joseph, take Mary as your wife. Soon she will have a baby, God's Son. He will grow up to help people become part of God's family. Name Him Jesus."

When Joseph woke up, he knew it was time for him and Mary to get ready for baby Jesus.

Based on Matthew 1:18-25; Luke 1:26-33
Value: Faith

Wise Men Follow a Star

Jesus was born in a little town called Bethlehem. Far away in a different country lived men who studied the stars. One night they saw a special new star. It was brighter than any they had seen before. It meant a king had been born.

The wise men eagerly made plans to visit this king! The star led them to Bethlehem and the house where little Jesus was living. The wise men bowed down to worship Him, and gave Jesus gifts fit for a king. Gold. Frankincense. Myrrh.

The wise men were happy as they traveled back to their country. They thanked God for sending a special star to help them find Jesus.

Based on Matthew 2:1-11
Value: Joyfulness

Jesus Finds Some Helpers

One day Jesus got into Peter and Andrew's boat so that all the people could hear Him talk about God. Later, when the people had left, Jesus told Peter to put the fishing nets into the water. "You'll catch a lot of fish," He said.

Peter and the other fishermen had not caught a single fish. But Peter said, "I will do what You say, Jesus." Suddenly, they caught more fish than the boat could hold. Peter and his brother had to call friends in another boat to help them pull in the fish.

Then Jesus said to Peter, "Come, be My helper! I will show you how to catch people for God." From that day, Peter and the other fishermen followed Jesus.

Based on Luke 5:1-11
Value: Helpfulness

The Lord's Prayer

Jesus was praying one day. When He was done, one of His helpers said, "Please teach us to pray."

Jesus began, "Call God 'Father.' God is like a father to all who love Him."

Then Jesus said, "You should tell God that you love Him. After that, you can ask for food and other things you need.

"You must also ask His forgiveness when you do wrong things. Ask Him to help you forgive others, too.

"And tell God when you need help saying 'No.' He will help you do what's right instead."

At the end of His lesson, Jesus said, "When you pray, don't give up. Keep asking God again and again for help. God will answer your prayers."

Jesus was glad that His helpers could talk to God just as He did.

Based on Matthew 6:9-13; Luke 11:1-4
Value: Prayerfulness

Calming a Storm

One day Jesus was teaching a crowd by the sea. Jesus stood in a boat so everyone could see Him. When it started to get dark, Jesus' helpers rowed the boat away from shore and Jesus lay down to sleep.

Suddenly the wind began to blow. Large waves tossed the boat. Jesus' helpers were so afraid that they woke Him up. Jesus stood and said to the wind and the waves, "Be still." The waves stopped moving. The wind stopped blowing. The boat stopped rocking. Everything was still!

Jesus asked, "Why were you afraid? Don't you know that I can help you?" Then His helpers knew they could trust Jesus to help whenever they were afraid.

Based on Mark 4:35-41
Value: Trust

Jesus Heals a Deaf Man

One day Jesus was traveling through the countryside. Some people brought a man to Him who could not hear. The man could not talk well, either. This man's friends had to give him special help. They begged Jesus to put His hands on the man and pray for him. They knew Jesus loved people who need special help.

Jesus took the man away for a while. He touched the man's ears and tongue. Then Jesus looked up to heaven and said, "Open up!" Suddenly the man could hear sounds. He could talk plainly too.

The man and his friends were so excited that they couldn't stop talking about what Jesus had done. They were glad that Jesus loved people who need special help.

Based on Mark 7:31-37
Value: Compassion

Jesus Loves
All the Children

Jesus was coming to town! Parents said, "Let's take our children to see Him." Everyone was excited, and when they saw Jesus walking down the road, the children ran to Him. They wanted to be close to Him.

Jesus' helpers said, "Go away! Jesus is too busy to see children now." The parents and children couldn't believe their ears. Sadly, they turned to go home.

But Jesus said, "Let the children come to Me. Do not send them away. I love children." The children ran to Jesus. He put His hands on their heads and prayed for them. Everyone was happy once more. They knew that Jesus loved them all. And they loved Jesus, too.

Based on Matthew 19:13-15
Value: Trust

The Good Samaritan

Jesus told this story to explain what kindness is.

One day a man was walking down a road. Some bad men robbed him and hurt him badly. Then they ran away.

A priest came down the road. Even though he was trained to be God's helper, he just walked by. A man called a Levite came down the road. Though he knew all God's rules by heart, he walked by without helping too.

Then a man from Samaria came down the road. The Samaritan stopped and helped the hurt man. After bandaging his wounds, he took the man to a hotel. "I will pay his bill until he gets well," he said.

Jesus said, "This is how we should treat other people."

Based on Luke 10:25-37
Value: Compassion

Zaccheus

The crowd was waiting to see Jesus. But Zaccheus was too short to see over other people's heads. So he climbed a tree to see Jesus coming down the road.

Jesus could see Zaccheus, too! As Jesus came nearer, He said, "Come down, Zaccheus. I am coming to your house today." Zaccheus climbed down the tree as quickly as he could.

Zaccheus told Jesus he was sorry for the wrong things he had done. "I will return anything I have stolen. And I will give half of my money to poor people."

Jesus was glad. He said, "This proves you really have changed. I came to help people like you. I care about you."

Based on Luke 19:1-10
Value: Repentance

A Basket Lunch

Jesus had been teaching the people for a long time. He noticed that they were getting very hungry. He told His helpers, "Feed the people."

"Where can we get that much food?" His helpers asked.

Andrew said, "This boy has some bread and fish in a basket."

Jesus took the bread and fish and said a prayer. Then He broke the food and passed it out to the people. Something wonderful happened! Even with so many people, there was plenty for everyone.

The people ate and ate. Then Jesus asked His helpers to collect the leftover food so nothing would be wasted. They collected twelve full baskets! Jesus used one little boy's lunch to feed everyone that day.

Based on John 6:1-14
Value: Faith

Lazarus Comes
Back to Life

Mary and Martha were sisters. They sent Jesus a message: "Come! Our brother, Lazarus, is sick!" But by the time Jesus came, Lazarus was dead.

Martha said, "If you had come sooner, Lazarus would be alive. But You can still help."

Jesus smiled. "Yes, I can help. Do you believe in Me, Martha?"

Martha said, "Yes, I believe, because You are God's Son."

Then Mary saw Jesus. She said, "If You had come sooner, Lazarus would be alive."

Jesus cried. He said, "Take Me to Lazarus."

At the tomb, Jesus prayed, "Thank You, God, for hearing Me. I want everyone here to know I am your Son." Then Jesus said, "Lazarus, come out!"

Lazarus was alive again! Mary and Martha had their brother back. And everyone knew Jesus had done something very special.

Based on John 11:1-44
Value: Compassion

Hosanna!
Jesus Is Our King

Jesus was on His way to Jerusalem. He asked two of His helpers to get a donkey for Him to ride.

Other people were going to the city too. They saw Jesus riding on the donkey. They remembered how Jesus had helped them. They wanted to show how much they loved Jesus. They would treat Him like a king!

Some people made a carpet of coats on the road. Others waved palm branches to show Him their love. Some sang, "Hosanna! You are our King!" The people were happy praising Jesus. Jesus was happy too.

Based on Matthew 21:1-11
Value: Praise

Jesus Says Good-bye

Jesus and His disciples were walking. It was late at night. Jesus said, "I am going away soon. When I am gone, love each other. Do all that I have told you."

Jesus said, "You are My friends, and that will get you into trouble. Some people will hate you just as they have hated Me. You must trust Me to help you when I go to be with My Father."

Jesus prayed for His disciples. "Father, My time on earth is over. Help My disciples. Keep them safe. They will tell others about You. Then others will believe that You sent Me. Someday all who believe will be with Me in heaven."

Based on John 15:9-22; 16:28-33; 17
Value: Courage

Jesus Dies For Us

Jesus was praying in a garden. Soldiers came with swords and spears to take Him away. The Jewish leaders wanted Jesus killed.

But Jesus did not fight to get away. He knew He had a special job only He could do. Jesus had come to earth to die in our place.

The soldiers took Him to the judge. The Jewish leaders said, "This man says He is God's Son. That's a crime!" Jesus did not deny it. He would have to die!

The soldiers put Jesus on a cross. Even though it hurt so much, Jesus said, "Father, forgive them. They don't know what they are doing!" Then He died. All His friends were sad. They did not know that Jesus died for them. They did not know that He would soon be alive again!

Based on John 18:1-11; 19:4-30
Value: Forgiveness

Mary Sees an Empty Tomb

Some people didn't believe Jesus was God's Son. They put Jesus on a cross, and He died. Then they took Jesus' body down and put it in a tomb, a cave carved out of rock, and rolled a stone in front of it.

Early on Sunday morning, Jesus' friend Mary went to the cave. But Jesus was not there! The stone was rolled to one side. Mary began to cry, "Someone has taken Jesus away."

Then Mary saw a man. She asked, "Where is Jesus?"

The man said softly, "Mary!"

Mary looked up. "Jesus!" she said. Jesus was alive again. Mary ran to find Jesus' friends. She shouted, "Jesus is alive! Jesus is alive!"

Based on Matthew 27:50, 57-60; John 20:11-18
Value: Joyfulness

Jesus Visits His Helpers

Jesus' helpers were afraid and hiding. Suddenly Jesus was in the room. "Peace be with you!" He said.

His helpers saw the nail marks in Jesus' hands and feet. Was it Jesus? Was He really there?

Jesus said, "Why do you doubt?" Jesus' helpers saw Him eat food. Then they knew He really was alive.

Thomas was not there. When the others told him what had happened, he did not believe Jesus was alive.

A week later Jesus came again and said, "Thomas, here are the nail marks. Do not doubt; just believe."

Thomas said, "Oh, Jesus, it IS You!"

Jesus said, "You believe I am alive because you see Me. How happy the people will be who believe without seeing Me!"

Based on Luke 24:36-43; John 20:19-29
Value: Joyfulness

Jesus Goes to Heaven

After Jesus came alive, He walked and talked and ate with His helpers. Jesus told them many things. Then He took them to a hill.

Jesus said, "Tell everyone in the small towns and the big cities about Me. Tell everyone in the world about Me. Tell them that I love them."

Suddenly, something wonderful happened. Jesus started to rise into the sky! A cloud covered Him. Two angels said, "Jesus has gone up to His home in Heaven. But He loves you. And someday, He will come back."

Jesus' helpers remembered that Jesus had said, "I am with you always." He was watching over them.

Based on Luke 24:50-53; Acts 1:7-11
Value: Purposefulness

God Rescues
Peter from Prison

Poor Peter! He was in prison because he loved Jesus. When Peter's friends heard the news, they met together to pray.

One night an angel came to the prison. The angel said, "Follow me." Peter obeyed, and the angel led him out through the prison gates. He was free!

Peter walked to the house of his friends. They were inside praying for Peter right at that moment. When he knocked on the door, a servant named Rhoda answered. Rhoda was so excited to see Peter, she forgot to let him in.

"Peter's at the door!" Rhoda shouted. But no one believed her.

Peter kept knocking until they let him in! Everyone thanked God for Peter's rescue. God answered their prayer.

Based on Acts 12:5-27
Value: Faith

A Miracle and a Mistake

Paul and Barnabas went to many places telling about Jesus. In one city they met a man who could not walk. While Paul talked about Jesus, he noticed the man's faith. Paul said to the man, "Stand up on your feet!"

The man stood up and walked around for the first time ever.

The crowd thought Paul and Barnabas had made the man well—not Jesus. "These men are gods!" they said. They wanted to worship Paul and Barnabas.

"Stop!" shouted Paul and Barnabas. "We are not gods! We are people like you. We have Good News to share about a real, living God."

Paul and Barnabas tried to explain, but the people did not understand. They could see Paul and Barnabas, but they could not see God. They wanted a god they could see.

Based on Acts 14:6-18
Value: Faith

Paul Tells People about Jesus

God sent Paul to the city of Corinth. Paul met a couple named Aquila (AK-wil-luh) and Priscilla. The three made tents to sell. But Paul's real job was preaching about Jesus.

Paul went to the synagogue to worship every week. (A synagogue was like a church for Jews.) Whenever he could, Paul preached in the synagogue that Jesus was God's Son.

Then Paul's helpers arrived. Timothy and Silas did many chores so Paul could spend all his time talking about Jesus. Even the leader of the synagogue believed in Jesus!

Many people wanted to stop the Christians. But God told Paul, "Don't be afraid. Speak out! Don't quit! I am with you, and no one can hurt you."

Paul taught in Corinth for more than a year. Then God sent him to other places.

Based on Acts 18:1-11
Value: Dedication

John Writes about God's Love

God told John to write a letter. John wrote, "God loves us very much. We know this because He sent Jesus to us. Now God calls us His children because we believe in His Son, Jesus. We are God's family, the church.

"Because of this, God does not want us to do wrong things. God wants us to love one another and do what is right. We can show our love for God by helping others in God's family."

God also sent John a special dream. John wrote down his dream: "God's family will live in heaven. We will stay there with Jesus forever. We can look forward to this because God's words are true."

Based on I John 3 and Revelation 21—22
Value: Love